My Book of Words

Illustrated by Heather Heyworth

Miles Kelly

At home

bedroom

curtains

bed

drawers

wardrobe

fridge

kitchen

cupboard

cooker

What colour are the curtains in the bedroom?

2

bathroom

toilet

sink

bath

television

window

door

sofa

lounge

How many of these objects have you got in your home?

3

In the home

cushion

lamp

clock

telephone

chair

book

table

Can you name the animal on the lamp?

Toys

teddy

car

jigsaw

train

doll

dinosaur

blocks

What are your favourite toys to play with?

5

In the garden

fence

shed

strawberries

carrots

bee

caterpillar

leaf

grass

dog

How many carrots are growing in the garden?

washing

bird

bush

ball

tree

butterfly

flowers

cat

What other things might be in a garden?

In the family

Grandad

Grandma

Daddy

Mummy

baby

sister

brother

How many people are there in this family?

My body

head

hair

ear

face

nose

mouth

eye

teeth

arm

tummy

hand

fingers

knee

leg

foot

toes

Can you point to these parts of your body?

On the street

park

bus

house

flats

bus stop

car

zebra crossing

motorbike

road

What colour is the car?

roof

shop

bicycle

pavement

pram

Which shops do you like best?

Things that go

aeroplane

hot-air
balloon

train

truck

tractor

How many of these vehicles can fly?

12

ambulance

helicopter

digger

ferry

fire engine

yacht

Which of these vehicles have you seen?

13

At the park

sky

kite

boat

path

pond

bicycle

ducks

picnic

ice cream

blanket

14

How many ducks can you see?

cloud

squirrel

bench

slide

swings

What do you like to do at the park?

Picnic food

bread

biscuits

cup

eggs

sandwiches

plate

cake

spoon

fork

knife

juice

16

How many different foods are in the salad?

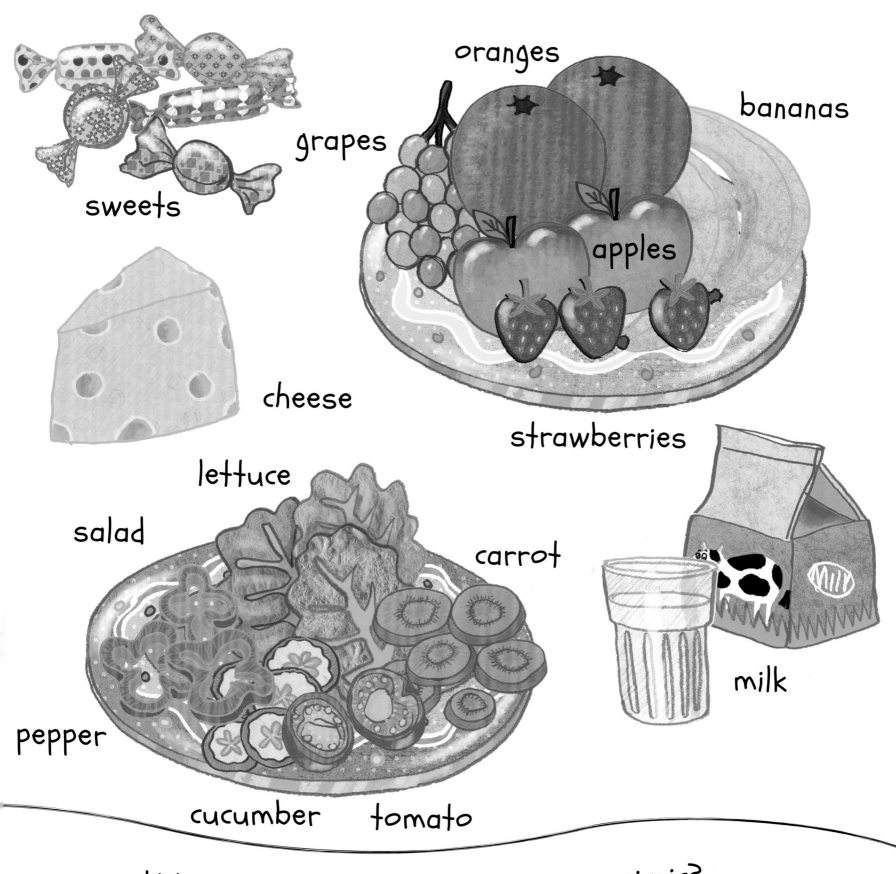

oranges

grapes

bananas

sweets

apples

cheese

strawberries

lettuce

salad

carrot

pepper

milk

cucumber   tomato

What food do you like to eat on a picnic?

On the beach

gull

boat

waves

spade

sandcastle

boy

bucket

shell

How many shells can you find?

What do you like doing on the beach?

Clothes

shorts

jumper

dress

t-shirt

socks

scarf

skirt

gloves

vest

pants

coat

shoes

trousers

Which of these clothes do you wear when it is cold?

Colours

black

green

yellow

blue

red

pink

brown

purple

orange

white

What colour clothes are you wearing?

Shapes

triangle

square

circle

rectangle

star

oval

diamond

heart

What shape is an egg?

Numbers

one
two
three
four
five
six
seven
eight
nine
ten

Can you count all the way from one to twenty?

Can you find?

Look back in your book to see if you can find the following things.

clock

teddy

dinosaur

hot-air balloon

yacht

sandwiches

sweets

t-shirt